POLISH MADONNAS

First published 1991, Warsaw.

Publishing House DAR
Dzierwa & Rosikoń
Aleja Dębów 4
05-080 Izabelin-Warsaw
Poland

Design: Michał Piekarski

Translated by Hanna Borowa-Szymańska

The authors want to thank Father Jan Golonka, OSPPE,
for his help in preparing this album, and particularly the
parts devoted to Our Lady of Częstochowa, and for
sharing the results of his studies into the copies of this
painting.
Consultation: Father Wiesław Kądziela

The authors supplemented the knowledge they gathered
during visits to St. Mary's sanctuaries with data included in
Father Wincenty Zaleski's book *Sanktuaria Polskie*.

Typesetting: Kazimierz Krzeski, Wspólna 69, Warszawa

Printed in Hong Kong

POLISH MADONNAS

JANUSZ ROSIKOŃ

TEXT WOJCIECH NIŻYŃSKI

INTRODUCTION FATHER MIECZYSŁAW MALIŃSKI

PUBLISHING HOUSE

DAR

Her images derive, like music, songs, architecture and customs, from our religious life but at the same time they are part of this life. This means that they not only express our religious feelings but also pass them on. Because in some way She is present in Her image through the faith which created Her, sketched Her figure, put the colours and decorated Her with gold and silver. The Christian religious life consists in a large degree in participating in the liturgical year — from Advent through Christmas, Lent, Easter to Pentecost. It is according to this rhythm that Her images are created.

In Advent, She is present like a Dawn Mass candle, expecting and announcing Her Son's arrival. She illuminates the darkness of man's solitude and fills him with hope for fruits of friendship between man and the Son of God.

There are other pictures depicting this part of her life. They are rare though. Only some painters had the courage to show the expectant Virgin. She appears on them to be still full of disbelief and fear about what has happened. And She also seems to anticipate the difficult matters before Her, the tasks which are almost impossible. What a superhuman mission She has to perform! But at the same time She looks happy and contemplates the mystery which is happening to Her.

There are few such pictures but all of them are rich in big meaning. Sometimes She is shown during the Visitation to St. Elizabeth, her relative who is also expecting a baby, the future John the Baptist. Sometimes the pictures show the two women in one another's arms.

And when Christmas comes, which begins with Christmas Eve dinners at homes and midnight masses at Churches, She is present in Carols. She is also important in Crechés displayed at all Churches and sometimes at homes too. She is the closest to the New Born Child. On His behalf, She accepts the adoration of the shepherds and the Magi. She carries Him in Her arms to the Temple. And She flees with Him and St. Joseph to Egypt.

The images of Madonna and Child are more frequent than other scenes from Her life. True, there are pictures of the stable at Bethlehem and Mary and Joseph bent over Jesus resting in the manger. Sometimes there are shepherds at their side, sometimes the Magi, or all of them together. There are some pictures belonging to the Adoration group on which not only the Magi but also the Holy Mother Herself pays tribute to Jesus. There are paintings of the Holy Family's escape to Egypt. On these, the Mother and Child are usually shown riding a donkey which is led by Joseph by the bridle. There are also pictures of Nazareth and of little Jesus helping Joseph in his carpenter's work under the Mother's watchful eyes.

But most frequently, the Holy Mother is shown holding Jesus in Her arms, Jesus who is strong enough to wear a royal crown on his head and hold a sceptre in his hand. Sometimes She bends over Him with great tenderness, looks at Him with loving eyes, or holds Him tight with affection. But most frequently She holds Him on Her arm and at the same time looks at those who come to Her and to Her Son. She looks at them with the eyes which are full of kindness as if She expected these visits and felt neither surprised nor frightened. And She waits to hear the good news of joy and success or the bad news of sorrow, trouble and tragedy. Nothing can surprise Her. She knows all these Herself, She has been through many difficult moments and is ready to speak even to God himself for the people who ask Her for this.

What comes next in the Liturgical calendar is the period of life in hiding in Nazareth, interrupted by twelve years' old Jesus getting lost in the Temple. And there She is present again with Her worry about the Son.

Such pictures are difficult to find. And the ones which we know of, usually show Mary and Joseph watching their Son talking to scribes, from behind a column or a gate.

According to the Gospel, Mary appeared again at Cana of Galilee at the time when Her Son was beginning His teachings. We remember Her saying there: „Whatsoever he saith unto you, do it." These words are addressed to the servants but we refer them to us. Because that was the beginning of His teachings.

These pictures are rare too: Jesus standing in the courtyard or a hallway with huge waterpots placed along the wall. And She is there at His side, full of concern and worry.

She does not accompany Him during His teachings. There is no such information in the Gospel. She reappears at the time of His Passion. She stands by the cross crying with the others. And this is how She appears at the time of Lent, as the Mother of the Dolours, the Sorrowful Mother, who is sharing His suffering. As the one in whose case Simeon's prophecy: „Yea, a sword shall pierce through thy own soul also" came true.

Some paintings show Mary under the cross on which Her Son Jesus is dying. She either stands there on Her own or is helped by John. Some other images depict Her with Christ's body on Her knees. Even in Poland these pictures are called Pietas. On other, less frequent occasions, the Sorrowful Mother is shown walking down Golgotha in a funeral procession following Her Son's Body carried by Joseph of Arimathaea, Nicodemus and John. Sometimes, we can also find pictures of the Holy Mother herself with her breast pierced by a sword, as was prophetised by Simeon.

The Gospel does not mention Her being present at the moment of Resurrection, but we know that she must have been there, or Her joy must have been there at least.

Neither does she witness her Son's Ascension. We meet Her again praying in the Cenacle on the day of Pentecost and see Her and the Apostles filled with Holy Ghost.

And this is how we see Her in the pictures, with flames above Her head and an inspired face.

In Polish Churches Her images are placed either at the central or the side altars. No, they are not placed, because she is not a thing, not just a picture. She has chosen those altars and found the best places for Herself and for Her Son. She does not want to rule, She wants to be the Mother to us in little rural Churches, fragrant with wax and incense and surrounded by lime trees, whose smell penetrates inside through the windows, the Churches where every Sunday not only the elderly women but also the young sing songs of devotion before the Holy Masses.

In the wooden mountain churches with shingle roofs, where the winters are long and the spring does not make haste to come.

In the urban churches, where the people bring similar concerns and troubles as the village people even though life is said to be easier in towns, but in fact it is even more difficult since street lamps overshadow the stars, asphalt squares replace the meadows and blocks of concrete eliminate the forests.

She has Her Feasts. But all Her great Feasts are connected with Her Son and His activity. Since even the Immaculate Conception was because of Him. And even the Assumption. And besides, She plays an important role not only at Christmas time but also in Christ's Passion, Death and Resurrection.

For us, She is the Servant of God and all Her Glory comes from Him. By venerating Her, we venerate Him who is responsible for Her great deeds.

When Her principal Feasts come, we undertake pilgrimages to find ourselves in person in those places which She has chosen, before those pictures in which She is present.

Apart from individual Feasts, we have devoted May, the loveliest of all months, to Her.

It is the month when cherry and apple trees cover themselves with a host of white flowers and when lilacs and jasmine begin to bloom. It is the time dedicated and offered to Her. It is the time of the Month–Of–May Devotions with the Loteran Litany sung in front of the Holy Sacrament.

And October, the month when the autumn displays its richness of colours, with its golden maple trees, red beeches and brown chestnuts popping out from their green thorny peels amidst the fallen leaves, is the time of the Rosary, an important form of prayers' recitations in the Catholic Church.

The Rosary helps us calm down the kaleidoscope of impressions, emotions and intellectual combinations and achieve silence, so that God, who is Silence, may enter into us and fill us with love and forgiveness, so that He who is Love may take us into His hands.

Whenever things went bad in Poland, the nation found support in its Mother. The nation clung to her to defend itself and survive. Our Lady of Kalwaria, Licheń, Kodeń, Piekary, Opole and a thousand other places always extended her protective cloak over those who were coming to her.

A special role has been and is played by Poland's most important Icon, Our Lady of Częstochowa. It was like that before and it is so now.

Let us trust Christ's Mother. Just as She helped us regain freedom, She will help us return to normality. But we must not stop coming to Her.

Father Mieczysław Maliński

▶ Częstochowa, Jasna Góra, Our Lady of Częstochowa (detail).

MAGNÆ MATRI VIRGINI
Eius vilissimum mancipium
Georgius Dux in Ossolin Sacri Rom. Imperij Princeps
Supremus Regni Cancellarius

Częstochowa (Częstochowa Diocese), **Our Lady of Częstochowa** also known as **Our Lady of Jasna Góra** or **Black Madonna**. This famous tempera painting on a lime panel is placed in the altar of a Gothic Chapel at the Jasna Góra Monastery. The Chapel contains a countless number of votive offerings. In its form, the image resembles a Byzantine icon. In accordance with its Church Doctrine, the whole East believed that a part of divine energy was contained by images representing the Divine Figures or Saints. Icons were actually manifestations of actual veneration of the figures they represented and hence the special adoration of these paintings.

A legend has it that Black Madonna was painted by St. Luke the Evangelist on a cypress panel coming from the table used by the Holy Mother in Nazareth. It was brought to Częstochowa from Jerusalem by Prince Władysław Opolczyk who presented it to the Pauline Monks on, as is generally believed, August 31, 1384. The picture was seriously damaged during a Hussite attack on the Monastery in 1430. Its restoration was commissioned personally by King Ladislaus Jagiełło (1351–1434) and the progress of restoration work was carefully described. The icon was somewhat "Polonaised" in the process. The scars on Madonna's face were left as evidence of its desecration.

The cultus of Our Lady of Częstochowa developed incessantly. The image was venerated by royal dynasties, noblemen, chivalry and ordinary people. In 1656, King John Casimir (1609–1672) chose Our Lady of Jasna Góra for the Patron of His Kingdom. In 1717, the image was decorated with crowns sent by Pope Clement XI. Black Madonna inspired many painters, poets and musicians from different epochs and played an important role in the Polish nation's moral revival, especially after World War II when the Great Novena was held at Primate Stefan Wyszyński's initiative and a copy of Black Madonna visited all parishes throughout Poland.

Jasna Góra is the most important of all St. Mary's sanctuaries in Poland. Located in the rare landscape of Jura Krakowsko--Częstochowska, the Jasna Góra Monastery and Church, surrounded by rectangular fortifications called *Fortalicium Marianum* and paths formed by pilgrims' processions, constitute a unique attraction. For centuries, this sanctuary has been the goal of countless pilgrimages. Also, congresses, conferences and meditations are held there. Copies of the image of Black Madonna are also venerated outside Poland. Principal celebrations fall on all Feasts of St. Mary. In 1931, Pope Pius XX proclaimed August 26 the Feast of Our Lady of Częstochowa.

Parczew (Siedlce Diocese), Madonna and Child frequently referred to as **Madonna with a Pear**. This is an early 17th century Flemish school painting. For many centuries it attracted members of the Catholic, Unite and Orthodox Churches. The picture was first placed in a Unite Church, next in an Orthodox Church and at present it hangs in the Roman Catholic Parish Church of St. John the Baptist. Principal celebrations fall on the Feast of the Assumption (August 15).

◀ **Kazimierz n. Wisłą (Lublin Diocese), The Annunciation.** Painted in the year 1600, the picture is a copy of an engraving by Hendrik Goltzius. It is the altarpiece at the Church of the Reformati. In the early 17th century its cultus was propagated by the Reformati Friars. According to an old chronicle, the number of votive offerings was so big in 1634 that they almost covered the entire altar. During the Swedish invasion of Poland in 1655, the picture was hidden on an island on the Vistula near Jaruntowice. Following the outbreak of the Kościuszko Insurrection (1794), the Reformati Friars donated all the votive offerings — 38 pounds of gold and sliver — to the nation for the supplies for the Insurrection Army. The picture was crowned on August 31, 1986, by Cardinal Franciszek Macharski. Principal celebrations fall on the Feasts of the Annunciation (March 25), the Immaculate Conception (December 8) and Our Lady of the Angels (August 2).

▶ **Sulisławice (Sandomierz–Radom Diocese), Our Lady of Sulisławice.** A late Gothic 15th century painting from the so-called Nowy Sącz School. It belongs to the *Misericordia Domini* iconographic category. It is today the altarpiece at the Church of the Birthday of Our Lady, but its story is very tangled. It had been a travel picture (its dimensions being 25cm x 25cm) and had been taken to wars by the Polish chivalry. On one such occasion it was taken to Ruthenia from where it was brought back to Poland by a Ruthenian girl taken captive by Wespazjan Rusiecki of Ruszcza. The pious girl prayed before the picture on her way to Poland and before her death in 1655 she presented it to the Church at Sulisławice where it at once became famous for miracles. An Ecclesiastical Commission examined the picture and confirmed its miraculous powers in 1659. Crowns were placed on it in 1913, in the presence of a congregation of 250,000 pilgrims from all over Poland. Principal celebrations fall on the Feast of the Birthday of Our Lady (September 8).

◀ **Opole (Opole Diocese), Our Lady of Opole.** A late 15th century painting on a lime panel placed at a side altar of St. Cross Cathedral. It was probably painted by a Bohemian artist. At first, the picture was placed at Piekary Śląskie from where, in 1680, it was taken to Prague at the request of Emperor Leopold I to protect the Czechs from plague. It was next twice brought to Opole and in 1702 remained there for good. This is one of the most beautiful representations of the Virgin Mary In Poland. On June 21, 1983, it was crowned personally by Pope John Paul II during a ceremony at Mt. St. Ann, the main sanctuary of the Opole Diocese. Principal celebrations fall on the Feast of the Exaltation of the Cross (September 14).

◀ **Gdańsk (Bołszowce) (Gdańsk Diocese), Madonna and Child (detail).** It is a copy of Lucas Cranach the Elder's famous painting "Madonna and Child under an Apple Tree" (now in the Ermitage in Leningrad). It was brought to Gdańsk from St. Catherine's Church in Cracow in 1966. Its cultus began in the early 17th century at the Carmelite Monastery at Bołszowce, the Lvov Archdiocese) where it was crowned at Pope Clement XIII's instruction on August 15, 1777. The picture was moved to Cracow in 1945. Principal celebrations fall on the Feast of Our Lady of the Scapular (July 16).

▶ **Rozprza (Częstochowa Diocese), Madonna and Child.** also known as **Our Lady of Consolation** The picture, now placed in the altar of the Church of the Visitation of Our Lady to St. Elizabeth, was for the first time included in the Church's inventory lists in 1676. Its cultus is of local character. Principal celebrations fall on the Feast of the Visitation (July 2).

Teratyń (Lublin Diocese), Our Lady of Consolation. A 17th century picture which had been venerated for years at the parish church in Zaturce, the Łuck Diocese, in Poland's former Eastern territory. After the war, the local people were displaced. They took the picture with them and placed it at The Church of St. Stanislaus at Teratyń where they found their new home. Principal celebrations fall on the Feast of Our Lady of Consolation (the last Sunday in August).

Lubecko (Katowice Diocese), Our Lady of Lubecko. The picture is placed in the retable of the Church of the Assumption. This small medallion (12.5cm x 7.5cm) is a copy of Our Lady of Częstochowa. On its back there is a picture of the face of Sorrowful Christ and the inscription *Ecce Homo*. Principal celebrations fall on the Sunday before the Feast of the Assumption. A traditional pilgrimage to Piekary Śląskie leaves Lubecko on that occasion.

Zembrzyce (Cracow Archdiocese), Our Lady of Zembrzyce. This panel painting is a slightly transformed copy of the famous Our Lady of Dublevo from a monastery in Moravia. Principal celebrations fall on the feast of Our Lady of the Scapular (July 16).

Kalwaria Zebrzydowska (Cracow Archdiocese). Our Lady of Kalwaria also known as The Crying Madonna. In the early 17th century, Cracow voivod Mikolaj Zebrzydowski ordered the building of several dozen small churches and chapels near Wadowice, thus creating the first ever shrine in Poland representing the Way of the Cross. The Bernardine Monks taking care of the place combined, in accordance with their tradition, the cultus of Jesus with that of the Mother of God, which became particularly strong after a miraculous image of The Crying Madonna was brought to Kalwaria bearing traces of tears of blood. The news about the miracle spread quickly, attracting large masses of pilgrims to the shrine. Today Kalwaria Zebrzydowska is the second biggest shrine in Poland after Częstochowa's Jasna Góra. The coronation of the Crying Madonna took place on August 15, 1887. Thousands of pilgrims arrive at Kalwaria Zebrzydowska every year to take part in special ceremonies commemorating the Holy Mother's Funeral and Triumph during the Holy Week and on the Feast of the Assumption (August 15).

Przemyśl Cathedral (Przemyśl Diocese), Madonna and Child also known as **Our Lady of St. Jack**. A Gothic statue in alabaster. It shows Madonna and Child sitting on a silver throne. A legend says that it was brought to Przemyśl by St. Jack Odrowąż after he fled Kiev before the Tartars. Whether this is true is rather dubious since art critics believe that the sculpture comes from the late 15th century. However, the present sculpture may be a copy of an original one placed at the Church by St.Jack. The first miracles and cures were recorded in Przemyśl in 1636.The sculpture was crowned in 1766. After the Dominican Monastery was closed in Przemyśl, it was moved to a side altar of the Basilica of the Virgin Mary and St. John the Baptist. Principal celebrations fall on the Feast of the Assumption (August 15).

▶ **Swarzewo (Chełm Diocese), Our Lady of Swarzewo** also known as **Fishermen's Madonna** and **The Star of the Sea**. This small 15th century Gothic statue sculpted in lime is placed in the central altar of the Church of the Birthday of Our Lady. A legend says that at the time of the Reformation it was thrown into the Baltic and next miraculously returned to Swarzewo. It is particularly venerated by fishermen and sailors who believe that it many times rescued them from drowning during storms. On August 28, 1937, the statue was crowned by Bishop Stefan Okoniewski. This is the only shrine to which pilgrims arrive by boats. Principal celebrations fall on the Feasts of Our Lady of the Scapular (16 July) and the Birthday of Our Lady (September 8).

▶ **Rywałd Królewski (Chełm Diocese), Our Lady of Rywałd** also known as **The Ruling Mary**. This Gothic sculpture from the late 14th century belongs to the Madonna on Lions circle. A legend has it that it was sculpted by an unknown Teutonic Knight from a castle in nearby Radzyń Chełmiński. The cultus developed at Rywałd in the 17th century. First mentions of miracles come from the year 1667. Parish chronicles contain a description of the case of a boy who suffocated and „was lying for four days showing no sign of life". The boy recovered after his parents dedicated him to Our Lady of Rywałd. Many similar cures were recorded at the sanctuary. It is taken care of by the Capuchin Friars. Between the wars the figure was particularly venerated by the Gypsies, the fact to which it owes the name of the Gypsy Queen. It was crowned on September 3, 1972, by Poland's Primate, Cardinal Stefan Wyszyński. It was a special moment for him since it was at the Rywałd Monastery that the Primate spent the first weeks after his imprisonment in 1953. Principal celebrations fall on the Feasts of the Visitation (May 31) and the Birthday of Our Lady (September 8).

Skępe (Płock Diocese), Madonna also known as **Our Lady of Skępe** and **the Queen of Mazovia**. The sculpture is placed in the central altar of the Church of the Annunciation. Skępe had been famous for miracles already in the mid 15th century. The place where the Mother of God appeared to the local people was the destination of many pilgrims asking for graces, including Castellan Kosztelecki's daughter who was cured there and, to show her gratitude, brought this Gothic lime sculpture from Poznań and placed it in the church founded by her Father. The splendour of our Lady of Skępe spread throughout the region. The sanctuary was among the most frequently visited ones in that part of Poland. The figure was crowned on May 18, 1755. A great number of votive offerings were presented to the Virgin over centuries. Principal celebrations fall on Pentecost and the Feast of the Birthday of Our Lady (September 8).

Szymanów (Warsaw Diocese), Our Lady of Jazłowiec (detail). The figure was sculpted in white Carrara marble by famous Polish sculptor Oskar Sosnowski for the Convent of the Immaculate Conception at Jazłowiec, Podolia. It was brought there in 1883 and quickly became an object of great veneration. During World War I a three-day battle was fought near the Convent. It was the first battle for an uhlan regiment which called itself the Jazłowiec Uhlans ever since and chose the statute of the Virgin Mary for their Hetman. Our Lady of Jazłowiec was crowned by Cardinal August Hlond on July 9, 1939, i.e., just before the outbreak of World War II. In 1946, the Nuns left Jazłowiec and took the statue with them. It was placed at a chapel at Szymanów near Warsaw. Principal celebrations take place there on the Feasts of Our Lady of Jazłowiec (July 9, i.e., the anniversary of the figure's coronation) and of the Immaculate Conception (December 8).

◀ **Płock (Płock Diocese), Our Lady of Mazovia.** A 17th century natural-size statue in white Carrara marble placed in the side altar of the Cathedral of the Assumption. Principal Celebrations fall on the Feast of the Assumption (August 15).

Gdańsk, St. Mary's Church. (Gdańsk Diocese), The Beautiful Madonna. The sculpture, placed in St. Reinhold's chapel in the northern nave of St.Mary's Basilica, comes from around the year 1410. It is a very skillful work both as far as its composition and elaborate details are concerned. Around 1520, the figure was put in a special case covered with reliefs and pictures, the fact which indicates that the Beautiful Madonna's cultus was popular as early as the beginnings of the 16th century. Only some parts of this case have been preserved till today. Celebrations fall on the Feast of the Assumption (August 15).

Piotrkowice (Kielce Diocese), Our Lady of Loreto. A Gothic sculpture from around the year 1400, placed at the Chapel of the Church of the Annunciation. The beginnings of its cultus date back to the 17th century when another figurine of the Virgin Mary was found in a nearby field and Our Lady showed herself to the local people. Already in 1630, an Ecclesiastical Commission examined the miracles and cures attributed to Our Lady of Loreto from Piotrkowice. At that time it was one of the most famous shrines in Poland. The statue was crowned by the Kielce Bishop, Czesław Kaczmarek, on September 7, 1958. Principal celebrations fall on the Feasts of the Annunciation (March 25), the Birthday of Our Lady (September 8), Our Lady of the Scapular (July 16) and Our Lady of Loreto (December 10).

▶ **Dębowiec (Przemyśl Diocese), Our Lady of La Salette**. The statue is placed in the local church. The cultus of Our Lady of La Salette originated in 1846 after the Holy Mother showed herself as the Beautiful Madonna to two little shepherds at the village of La Salette. She was sitting and crying with her face hidden in her hands. The fame of this miraculous appearance quickly spread outside the borders of France. At the outset of the present century, La Salette Missionaries arrived at Dębowiec where they at once started propagating St. Mary's cultus. Miraculous sculpture of the Crying Madonna is placed in a church built by these Missionaries at Dębowiec. Celebrations in honour of Our Lady of La Salette fall on the third Sunday of May and the third Sunday of September.

Stęszew (Poznań Archdiocese), Immaculate Virgin. A legend has it that this 16th century sculpture comes from a wooden church burnt by the heretics. Only the figure survived the fire but when it was placed in a different church it miraculously returned to the old church's debris. This translocation was interpreted as asign from God and a new church was built at Stęszew. The cultus of St. Mary, which developed there very quickly, is evidenced by descriptions of numerous votive offerings and books of miracles all of which were lost during World War II. Principal celebrations fall on the Feast of the Immaculate Conception (December 8).

▶ **Międzygórze (Wrocław Archdiocese), Madonna and Child.** The sculpture was brought to Międzygórze in 1750 from a known St. Mary's sanctuary at Mariazell, Austria. Chiselled in lime wood, it is not a faithful copy of the Austrian original and has many features characteristic of the 18th century Silesian art. The sculpture was placed on Mt. Igliczna (847 m. above the sea level) where quite soon a chapel was built under the invocation of Our Lady of the Snows. This is the highest situated sanctuary of the Virgin Mary in Poland. Many miraculous cures were recorded there especially from eye diseases. Quite recently the Mt. Igliczna Madonna has been named the Patron of Sportsmen. Pope John Paul II crowned the figure in Wrocław on June 21, 1983, during his second pilgrimage to Poland. Principal celebrations fall on the Feast of Our Lady of the Snows (August 5).

◀ **Tulce (Poznań Archdiocese), Our Lady of Tulce.** A late Gothic sculpture from around the year 1500, chiselled in lime and polychromed. It is placed at the central altar of the Church of the Birthday of Our Lady. The three leaning figures symbolise Mankind looking with hope towards the Holy Mother. On September 2, 1979, the Poznań Metropolitan Archbishop, Jerzy Stroba, decorated Madonna and Child with Papal crowns. Principal celebrations take place at Tulce on the Feasts of the Visitation (May 31) and Our Lady of Consolation (the last Sunday in August).

◀ **Ludźmierz (Cracow Archdiocese), Our Lady of Ludźmierz** also known as **The Queen of Podhale**. A magnificent statue from the first half of the 14th century. It is one of the Beautiful Madonnas sculpted by an artist from the Nowy Sącz School. The statue is now placed in the central altar of the Church of the Assumption. According to a 1592 mention in the church records the statue had long been known for its miraculous powers and decorated with crowns. Since times immemorial, it has been called the Queen of Podhale. Mountaineers from far away places, including Spis and Orava, have made pilgrimages to this shrine. On August 15, 1963 the statue was crowned by Cardinal Stefan Wyszyński. An incident — which years later was interpreted as prophetic — took place on that occasion. Four bishops were carrying down the stairs a feretory with Our Lady of Ludźmierz. At one moment the statue swayed and the sceptre slipped from Mary's hand. At the last moment it was caught by the then young Bishop Karol Wojtyła. The witnesses of that event remembered it after Cardinal Wojtyła was elected the Pope to become the Head of the Catholic Church. Celebrations take place at Ludźmierz on almost all Feasts of the Virgin Mary.

Leśniów (Częstochowa Diocese), Our Lady of Leśniów also known as **The Patron of Families**. This late 14th century sculpture is placed in the central altar of the Pauline Monks' Church. A legend says that it was brought to Silesia from Ruthenia by Prince Wladyslaw Opolczyk. Feeling thirsty, he stopped at Leśniów but there was no water around. He started to pray and a spring appeared just at his side. He ordered that a chapel be built there and placed the figure in it. In 1706, the chapel was entrusted to the care of the Pauline Monks. On August 13, 1967, the figure was crowned by Primate Stefan Wyszyński assisted by Cardinal Karol Wojtyła. According to Polish Liturgical Calendar the Feast of Our Lady of Leśniów falls on July 2.

Głogówek (Opole Diocese), Our Lady of Loreto. A Baroque sculpture from the first half of the 17th century placed at the so–called Loreto House at the side chapel of the Franciscan Church. In the late 16th and early 17th centuries the building of Loreto Houses was popular in the whole of Europe. This custom derived from the belief that angels carried the real house of St. Mary from Nazareth to Loreto. Many such houses were built in Poland and the house at Głogówek is one of them. It attracted numerous pilgrimages, particularly from Silesia. Celebrations fall on the Feasts of the Annunciation (March 25), Portiuncula (August 2) and St. Francis (October 4).

Sejny (Łomża Diocese), Madonna and Child also known as **Our Lady of Sejny.** The sculpture is placed in the altar of a chapel of the post–Dominican Church of the Visitation. This is an extremely interesting example of the so–called cabinet Madonna, only a few of which have been preserved in Europe until the present day. When closed, it shows the Holy Mother sitting on a throne and upon its opening it reveals a triptych with a Gothic representation of the Holy Trinity. The central relief shows the Father holding a cross with crucified Christ and the Holy Spirit represented as a dove. The painted side panels depict the figures of kneeling men and women who are looking for protection under the Holy Mother's cloak. The sculpture was brought to Sejny from Konigsberg at the end of the 16th century. Poles, Lithuanians and Ruthenians alike made pilgrimages to this shrine, recognising in St. Mary these nations' common mother. The sculpture was crowned by Cardinal Stefan Wyszyński on September 7, 1975.

Miejsce Piastowe (Przemyśl Diocese),
Madonna and Child. The sculpture is placed in the side altar of the Church of the Visitation. It is a masterpiece of Gothic art from the third quarter of the 14th century. This kind of Madonnas was popular in Małopolska, Spis and Bohemia and similar representations of the Virgin can be found in the churches at Szaflary, Lipniki, Nowy Sącz and the Carmelite Convent in Cracow. Regrettably, the figure was damaged in the process of restoration at the beginning of this century. The hands and the figure of the Child were cut off from the sculpture. The whole work was covered by a wooden dress attached to the Gothic figure with screws. The present figure of the Child is a copy of the original one which was lost in the meantime. The figure's former cultus almost died out today. Celebrations are nevertheless held at the church on the Feasts of the Immaculate Conception (December 8), the Assumption (August 15) and the Birthday of Our Lady (September 8).

Lubaczów (Archdiocese in Lubaczów),
Our Lady of Grace. The picture was painted by burgher Józef Wolfowicz from Lvov after the death of his granddaughter. It soon became famous for miracles. In 1656, it was moved to the Lvov Cathedral, where on April 1 of that year King John Casimir (1609—1672) attended a high mass during which, in the presence of the court, chivalry and Senators, he read out a vow dedicating the Polish and

Lithuanian nations and state to the protection of the Virgin. It was then that Our Lady was given the title of the Queen of the Kingdom of Poland. On May 12, 1776, the picture was crowned for the first time. Its second coronation took place at Częstochowa's Jasna Góra Monastery during Pope John Paul II's 1983 pilgrimage to Poland. Principal celebrations fall on the Feast of Our Lady, the Queen of Poland (May 3).

Łódź, The Church of Assumption (Łódź Diocese),
Our Lady of Łódź also known as **Our Lady of Bałuty**. The picture is placed in the altar of a side chapel. The 1753 church records mention the picture's miraculous powers and 18th century votive offerings have been preserved till today. Principal celebrations fall on the Feast of the Assumption (August 15).

Kodeń (Siedlce Diocese), Our Lady of Kodeń also known as **The Queen and the Mother of Podlasie**. It is the altarpiece at St. Ann's Church. The painting originally belonged to Pope Urban VIII and it was in front of it that Mikołaj Sapieha, also known as Mikołaj the Pious, was cured during his pilgrimage to Rome. Sapieha asked to be given the picture. After he met with the Pope's refusal, he abducted it and on September 15, 1631, brought the painting to Kodeń where he first placed it at his castle chapel and later ordered that it be moved to St. Ann's Basilica. Initially, the Pope threatened to excommunicate him but after Sapieha's second pilgrimage to Rome he pardoned him and eventually let him have the painting. Its cultus developed very quickly. On August 15, 1723, crowns were brought to Kodeń from St. Peter's Chapter at the Vatican and placed on the image with Pope Clement XI's approval. That was the third instance of a painting's coronation in Poland. After the fall of the January Insurrection (1863), the painting was taken to the Jasna Góra shrine in Częstochowa from where it returned to Kodeń in 1927, entrusted to the Oblate Missionaries. Principal celebrations take place at Kodeń on the Feasts of the Assumption (August 15), the Birthday of Our Lady (September 8) and on the anniversary of bringing the picture to Kodeń (September 15).

Radomyśl (Przemyśl Diocese), The Sorrowful Mother. A late 16th century painting. According to a local legend, a tradesman floating timber on the San River was miraculously rescued during a flood in 1625. To thank the Virgin for his deliverance, he built a chapel on a hill called *Zjawienie* and placed the picture in it. Today the chapel is surrounded by a cemetery. A Golden Book of *Zjawienie* preserved at the chapel lists numerous miracles, rescues and cures attributed to the Sorrowful Mother. Celebrations fall on the Feasts of Our Lady of Consolation (Sunday after August 28) and The Sorrowful Mother (Friday before Palm Sunday).

Maków Podhalański (Cracow Archdiocese),
Our Lady of Maków also known as **The Patron or The Queen of Families** owing to the graces bestowed on whole families arriving at this shrine. It is the altarpiece at the Church of the Transfiguration. The painting was commissioned in 1590 by Parish Priest Wojciech Dąbski. The cultus of the Virgin Mary at Maków dates back to the early 17th century. It was before this picture that the Cracow Metropolitan Bishop, Adam Sapieha, dedicated the whole Cracow Diocese to the Immaculate Heart of the Virgin Mary in 1946. On June 10, 1979, the last day of his first pilgrimage to Poland, Pope John Paul II crowned the picture during a ceremony at the Cracow greens. Celebrations fall on the Feast of the Immaculate Conception (December 8).

▶ **Stara Wieś (Przemyśl Diocese), Our Lady of Mercy**. The picture features the Dormition and the Assumption of Our Lady. It is a faithful copy of an early Renaissance painting which was burnt in 1968 and which had once constituted the central part of a triptych. It was the Pauline Monks who most strongly contributed to the development of the cultus of Our Lady of Stara Wieś. The origins of this cultus date back to the 15th century. In the mid–19th century the sanctuary was taken over by the Jesuits. For centuries, the picture has attracted many pilgrims not only from Poland but also from Slovakia and Hungary. On September 8, 1877, Papal crowns were placed on it. This was the first instance of a picture's coronation in 19th century Poland. After the picture burnt in a fire, its copy was painted and was crowned by Cardinal Stefan Wyszyński in 1972. Principal celebrations fall on the Feasts of the Assumption (August 15) and the Birthday of Our Lady (September 8).

◀ **Piotrków Trybunalski (Łódź Diocese), Our Lady of Piotrków.** This late Gothic image of the Dormition of Our Lady comes from the first quarter of the 16th century. Many features of this painting are similar to those of a fragment of the famous Veit Stoss altar from St. Mary's Church in Cracow and of the miraculous image of Our Lady of Stara Wieś. According to some early mentions, the picture was presented to the Piotrków Church by Queen Bona (1494—1557), the fact which made Piotrków burghers pray for her soul on every eve of All Saints' Day. The image was proclaimed miraculous by a special Bishops' Decree in 1659. It was the object of great veneration at that time, but today the cultus has almost disappeared so that no celebrations are held at the parish on St. Mary's feasts.

▶ **Rokitno (Warsaw Archdiocese), Madonna and Child** also known as **Our Lady of Rokitno (detail).** It is the altarpiece at St. Jacob's Church. The 1702 and 1703 parish records mention three miraculous recoveries in front of the picture. The Bishop of Kiev, Józef Andrzej Załuski, himself wrote: "Rokitno near Warsaw: I experienced a miracle there and on foot carried my votive offering to it." Poland's Primates frequently stopped at Rokitno on their way to Gniezno or Łowicz. Some 17th and 18th century votive offerings are still at the Church, some others were donated to help the country following the 1794 National Government's appeal. Principal celebrations fall on the Feasts of the Assumption (August 15) and the Birthday of Our Lady (September 8).

Chłopice (Przemyśl Diocese), Our Lady of Chłopice. The story of this shrine is connected with a colourful legend about a horse trader. One day, when he was taking his horses for sale, they ran away to the Chłopice forest. The trader found them a short time later kneeling on their front legs before a wild pear tree. When the man looked up he saw the face of the Virgin Mary among the branches. He built a chapel there with the pear tree's trunk in the altar. The picture was brought to Chłopice in 1684. Some original frescoes illustrating the miracles attributed to Our Lady of Chłopice between 1506 and 1867 have been preserved on the chapel's walls. Principal celebrations fall on the Feast of the Visitation (July 2).

◀ **Gąsawa (Gniezno Archdiocese), Our Lady of Consolation (detail)**, the Patron of regular Lateran Canons. The picture is placed in the central altar of the Church of St. Nicolas. It is probably a 17th century copy of a picture found in Borek Polski, one of the oldest sanctuaries of Our Lady of Consolation in Poland. Principal celebrations fall on the Feast of the Immaculate Conception (December 8) and Our Lady of Consolation (August 27).

Pajęczno (Częstochowa Diocese), Madonna and Child. This early 16th century picture is the altarpiece at the Church of the Assumption. Its cultus developed early and in the 17th century the picture was officially announced to have miraculous powers. Poet Wespazjan Kochowski described it in one of his epics. Numerous old votive offerings have been preserved till today. Principal celebrations fall on the Feasts of the Assumption (August15) and the Birthday of Our Lady (September 8).

**Nieznamierowice
(Sandomierz–Radom Diocese),
Our Lady of the Holy Family**.
A low relief at the Church of St.
Andrew the Apostle. At first a
picture, which at present is an
object of a cultus at nearby
Studzianna, was venerated at
Nieznamierowice. After it was
removed from there, the cultus
of Our Lady of the Holy Family
did not die down. So when a
new church was being built there
between the Wars, the Parish
Priest turned to sculptor
Wincenty Bogaczyk, a disciple
of Xawery Dunikowski, to carve
a relief which would be a faithful
copy of the miraculous picture
from Studzianna. Principal
celebrations fall on the Feasts of
St. Joseph (March 19) and St.
Andrew (November 30).

Studzianna (Sandomierz-Radom Diocese), Our Lady of Studzianna also known as Our Lady of The Holy Family. This painting, representing the Holy Family at en evening meal, was brought to Poland from Germany in 1637 as Emperor Ferdinand II's gift for his daughter Cecilia Renata, after she wedded Polish King Ladislaus IV (1595—1648). Lost and recovered many times, the picture was eventually placed at the Studzianna Church where it quickly became famous for miracles. In 1671, a special Ecclesiastical Commission proclaimed it a miraculous image. The Philippian Friars, who arrived at Studzianna three years later, have ever since taken care of the sanctuary. In 1968, Cardinal Stefan Wyszyński coronated the picture. Principal celebrations fall on almost all feasts of St. Mary.

Cracow, Carmelite Church (Cracow Diocese),

Madonna and Child. also known as **Our Lady of the Sands**, the name which is attributed to the fact that it is placed at the Carmelite Church *Na Piasku* (On the sand). A legend says that a monk was painting the image of the Virgin Mary on the Church's outside wall. When the bells summoned the monks for evening prayers, he left the work unfinished. When he wanted to resume painting the next morning, he found the image completed. Art restorers agree that the fresco was probably a part of a larger composition. The cultus of Our Lady of the Sands began in the 17th century and intensified after the image survived the destruction of the Church by the Swedes. It is traditionally believed that the scars on Our Lady's face were formed at that time. Many Polish kings stopped to pray at the sanctuary, including King John III Sobieski (1629–1696) before his Vienna expedition. The painting was crowned on May 8, 1883, and the crowns were designed personally by Jan Matejko (1838–1893). One interesting iconographic aspect of the image is the unusual depicting of the Mother of God as an elderly matron rather than a young woman. Principal celebrations fall on the Feasts of the Visitation (May 31), Our Lady of the Scapular (July 16) and the Birthday of Our Lady (September 8).

Paczółtowice (Cracow Archdiocese), Our Lady in Olive Grove. A panel painting from around 1470 ascribed to a Cracow workshop. It was once a part of a triptych with the other two parts representing St.Catherine and St. Barbara. Today the central part is the altarpiece while the two side panels are placed on both sides of the central altar. Numerous votive offerings indicate that the picture had been strongly venerated in the old times.

▶ **Lublin (Lublin Diocese), Madonna and the Child.** also known as **Our Lady of Latyczów (detail)**. The picture was blessed by Pope Clement VIII and brought to Latyczów, Podolia, from Rome by the Dominican Friars. Placed in a provisional chapel, it emanated supernatural light, and soon became famous for conversions and miracles giving rise to a cultus which flourished throughout Podolia. The Virgin gave many proofs of her protection of Latyczów and many victories over Cossack and Tartar detachments were attributed to her. Many wars and invasions made the picture frequently change its place, to mention Lvov, Winnica, Warsaw and Łuck. After World War II it was brought to Lublin and placed in a chapel of the Convent of the Immaculate Conception. The picture, which in 1636 had already been honoured with a big number of votive offerings of great value, was crowned in 1778 on the basis of a decree issued by Pope Pius VI. Celebrations fall on the Feast of our Lady of Latyczów (July 2)

Strabla (Diocese in Drohiczyn), Our Lady of Strabla. The first mention of the picture is included in a 1617 inventory. It refers to a wooden chapel at Strabla and a „Moscow folding picture of Our Lady, covered with gold–plated silver". This indicates that this small 32cm x 27cm icon, painted on canvass and spread on a limepanel, was brought to Poland from the East in the late 16th or early 17th century. With the exception of the Virgin's face, the rest of the painting is covered by a robe of a silver sheet with a repousse plant ornament. The 1770 parish records mention numerous votive offerings brought to Our Lady of Strabla. Today her cultus is local in character.Celebrations fall on the Feast of the Ascension.

◄ **Warsaw, Dominican Friars' Church, (Warsaw Diocese). Madonna and Child.** This picture of the Immaculate Virgin of the Rosary had been venerated from the mid 16th century at the Dominican Friars Church at Żółkiew near Lvov. The picture was treated with special reverence by Żółiew's owner, Hetman Stanislaw Żółkiewski (1547—1620), and for thirteen years was among the possessions of King John Casimir (1609—1672), who even sought consolation in it when in exile during the Swedish invasion of Poland (1655). The crown was placed on the picture in 1929. After World War II, the picture was brought to Warsaw and deposited with the Dominican Friars' Church in Warsaw's Służewiec District. Principal celebrations fall on the Feast of the Rosary (October 7).

Leśna Podlaska (Siedlce Diocese), Our Lady of Leśna. A 17th century low relief in red stone, apparently polychromed in the past. It belongs to the iconographic category of Our Lady of the Holy Spirit and is a work of a folk artist. The story of this relief dates back to 1683, when two little shepherds saw the radiating image of the Madonna on a wild pear tree. Crowds of people began to gather there soon after. A year later, a Bishops' Commission issued a decree confirming the relief's supernatural properties. It was placed in a specially erected church. In 1700, the Bishop of Łuck permitted the relief's public veneration. The cultus developed quickly, which is evidenced by numerous magnificent voting offerings including a votive robe of pure gold, decorated with 155 diamonds, 291 rubies and 59 emeralds offered to Our Lady of Leśna by Countess Anna Radziwiłł. Since 1727, the sanctuary at Leśna Podlaska has been cared for by the Pauline Monks. The relief was crowned on August 18, 1963, by Cardinal Stefan Wyszyński. Principal celebrations fall on the Feast of the Visitation (September 8) and Pentecost.

**Łask (Łódź Diocese),
Our Lady of Łask**. A late 15th
century tondo–shaped low
relief in alabaster. It is placed at
the chapel of the Church of the
Visitation and St. Michael. The
relief is a work of Italian
Renaissance sculptor Andrea
della Robi. It was presented to
Poland's Primate Jan Łaski by
the Pope during the 5th Lateran
Council. After his return to
Poland, the Primate gave it to a
newly built Church at Łask, his
hometown. It is placed today in
a special chapel in a ray–shaped
frame containing relics of the
Saints. Celebrations fall on the
Feast of the Immaculate
Conception (December 8).

Warsaw (Warsaw Archdiocese), Madonna and Child also known as **the Guardian of Poland and the Victorious Hetman**. The picture is placed in the Dominican Church of St. Jack in Warsaw's Old Town. Brought to Poland after World War II, it had been venerated for over three centuries at a Dominican Church at Cortkov on the Seret (former Tarnopol Voivodship). It resembles the famous image of Our Lady of Tuchów. According to a prayer printed on the picture's pre-war copies, the Cortkov painting was presented to the local church by King John Casimir (1609–1672). The faithful gather before the picture on every first Sunday of September.

▶ **Szczyrzyc (Tarnów Diocese), Our Lady of Szczyrzyc (detail).** An inscription in the 18th century *Inventorium Cirzickiego Kosciola* indicates that the faithful were bringing numerous votive offerings to this picture to thank for graces bestowed on them by the Virgin Mary. A 1728 mention in the Church Chronicle refers to 51 precious votive offerings. The cultus declined after Poland's partitioning by foreign powers and was restored as late as the mid–20th century. Among those who made pilgrimages to Our Lady of Szczyrzyc was famous actor Juliusz Osterwa. The picture was crowned on August 19, 1984, by Cardinal Józef Glemp. Principal Celebrations fall on the Feasts of St. Stanislaus (May 8) and St. Bernard (August 20).

Racibórz (Opole Diocese), Our Lady of Racibórz. This late 16th century panel paining is a copy of the miraculous image of Our Lady of Jasna Góra. A legend has it that a Racibórz inhabitant, who was miraculously cured by the Virgin, made a thanksgiving pilgrimage to Częstochowa and brought this picture back with him. The Racibórz sanctuary is the oldest centre of St. Mary's cultus in Upper Silesia. Known for numerous miracles and graces, the picture was crowned by the Archibishop of Wrocław, Cardinal Adolf Betram, in 1932, during a ceremony commemorating the 500th anniversary of the cultus of our Lady of Racibórz. Principal celebrations fall on the Feasts of the Assumption (August 15) and the Birthday of Our Lady (September 8).

◄ **Będków (Łódź Diocese), Our Lady of Będków (detail).** A late 15th or early 16th century altarpiece at the Church of the Birthday of our Lady. It is likely that the picture was presented by Queen Bona to her relative from the Spinka family which owned Będkow. But first mentions of the picture come from as late as 1717. In 1770, the Archbishop of Gniezno, Gabriel Podolski, confirmed the picture's miraculous powers following its examination by a special Ecclesiastical Commission. Its cultus was very widespread — from 1771 to 1775 alone, 181 instances of cures and miracles were recorded there. Principal celebrations fall on the Feast of the Birthday of Our Lady (September 8).

Kurozwęki (Sandomierz–Radom Diocese), Madonna and Child also known as **Our Lady of the Heart**. It is the altarpiece at the Church of the Assumption and St. Augustine. This Baroque 17th century picture was brought to Kurozwęki in 1648 by Anna Lanckorońska who received it from the Pope during her pilgrimage to Rome for her service to the Church. The picture, which was widely venerated from the beginning, is decorated with a silver dress, valuable crowns and rings placed on the Virgin's fingers. Principal celebrations fall on the Feast of the Assumption (August 15).

Białystok (Białystok Archdiocese), Our Lady of Mercy. The image was painted in 1927 by Łucja Bałzukiewiczówna. It is a faithful copy of the famous icon of Our Lady of Ostra Brama (The Pointed Gate) which has been venerated in Vilnius since the 17th century. The Ostra Brama image was crowned on July 2, 1927, and the copy was painted to commemorate that occasion. After World War II, when the state borders were shifted and thus changed the shape of the Vilnius Archdiocese, the people from the Białystok region could no longer make pilgrimages to Vilnius. Hence the special veneration of the copy placed at the Białystok Procathedral. In 1977, on the 50th anniversary of the memorable Vilnius coronation, Cardinal Karol Wojtyła consecrated the chapel where the picture was placed. Principal celebrations fall on the Feast of the Assumption (August 15).

Wrocław Jesuit Church (Wroclaw Archdiocese), Our Lady the Helper. It is a faithful copy of Lucas Cranach's painting. The sources of this iconographic category of St.Mary's images are highly interesting. Confraternities of Our Lady the Helper of Christians were popular at the time of strong religious movements in the 16th and 17th centuries. The *Auxilatrix Cristianorum* motif entered a new phase following the victory over the Turks in 1571 and became the synonym of Victorious Madonna. The first Confraternity of the Helper of Christians was founded in the German Empire during the Thirty Years' War by a group venerators of the image of Madonna painted by Cranach. Similar Confraternities were founded later on in other countries, including Poland, as a manifestation of Counter–Reformation. This was how the cultus of Our Lady the Helper reached the Jesuit Church in Wrocław. The painting belonged to Countess Katarzyna Dworzak who, upon her death, presented it to Countess Maria Zarub, Baroness Lissar, who, in turn, handed it over to the Jesuits. No special celebrations are held at the Church in connection with the Feasts of St. Mary.

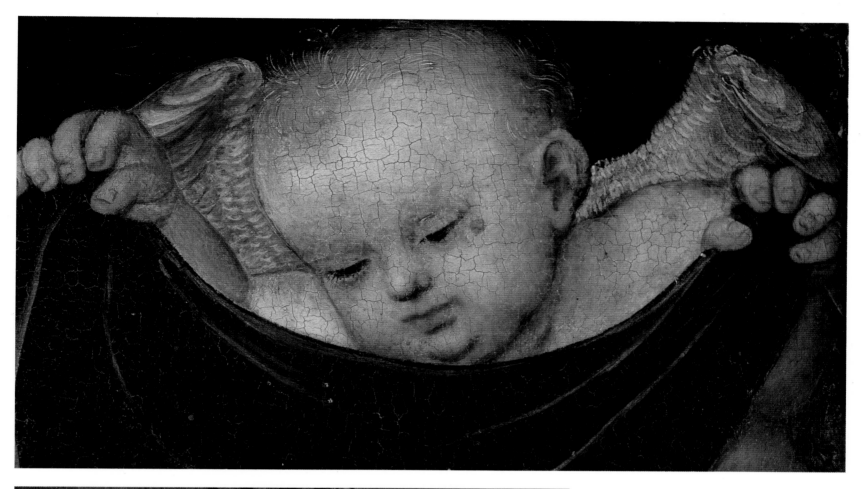

Sulmierzyce (Częstochowa Diocese),
Our Lady of Sulmierzyce. This miraculous picture was probably brought to Poland from Rome in the second half of the 16th century. Parish chronicles ascribe it to Cranach but do not say whether it was Cranach the elder or the younger who painted it. It may be presumed that the picture was painted in their workshop or is a work of one of their disciples. In 1666, a special bishops' decree proclaimed it to have miraculous powers. During World War II, the Nazis turned the local church into a grain store. Saved by miracle from destruction, the painting hang all the war long in the office of the Ordinary Bishop of Częstochowa, Teodor Kubina, and returned to the Church of St. Erasmus at Sulmierzyce after Poland's liberation. It was placed in the Church's side altar. Principal celebrations fall on the first Sunday of October in connection with the Feast of Our Lady of the Rosary (October 7).

◀ **Skrzyńsko (Sandomierz–Radom Diocese),**
Our Lady of Stare Skrzyńsko.
A panel painting from the turn of the 15th century placed at the central altar of St. Adalbert's Church. The cultus of Our Lady of Stare Skrzyńsko reached its climax in the 18th century. A legend included in Jan Długosz's (1415–1480) Chronicles says that the Church's founder Piotr Dunin, who had had his eyes hollowed out and his tongue cut off, regained them while praying before the painting. Principal celebrations fall on the Feasts of Our Lady of the Scapular (July 16) and the Birthday of Our Lady (September 8).

◀ **Kępa Polska (Płock Diocese), Our Lady of Kępa.**
It is the altarpiece at the local church. The Cultus of Our Lady of Kępa dates back to the 17th century. A legend says that the construction of the Church at Kępa was connected with the finding of this miraculous picture. One day, local fishermen found it floating on the Vistula against the river's current. They recovered it and placed in a small wooden wayside chapel. Soon, the picture was found to emanate unusual light. A church was built then at the site where the picture was originally placed. Many cures and miracles were recorded before Our Lady of Kępa. Votive offerings, attached directly to the picture, have been preserved till now. Principal celebrations fall on the Feasts of the Annunciation (March 25) and the Birthday of Our Lady (September 8).

▶ **Rymanów (Przemyśl Diocese). Our Lady of Rymanów.**
According to a local legend, this expressive picture of the Sorrowful Mother pierced with a sword, with Christ bleeding at her feet, was presented to the local church by King Ladislaus Jagiełło (1351–1434). But art critics maintain that the picture comes from the mid-16th century. Already in the 18th century it was widely recognised for cures and its cultus has continued until the present day. Principal celebrations fall on the Feasts of the Sorrowful Mother (September 15) and of the Rosary (October 7).

▶ **Odporyszów (Tarnów Diocese), Our Lady of Odporyszów**. The picture the altarpiece is the Church of the Purification. It was presented to the Church by the Dębinski family in 1570. The cultus of the Virgin Mary began at Odporyszów in the mid–17th century and intensified after the Swedish invasion, when the Holy Mother showed herself to the local people in a nearby forest and promised to protect them against foreign troops. Since 1905, the sanctuary has been entrusted to the care of St. Vincent a Paulo Missionaries. It was decorated with Papal Crowns in 1937. One old form of venerating Our Lady at Odporyszów are mystery plays imitating the Calvary ceremony of Our Lady's Funeral and the Assumption. Principal celebrations fall on the Feasts of the Mother of the Church (2nd day of Pentecost) and the Birthday of Our Lady (week–long celebrations).

◀ **Dubiecko (Przemyśl Diocese), Our Lady of Dubiecko**. A folk artists who painted this picture at the turn of the 16th century used for his model a miraculous figure from the Jesuit Church at Jarosław. The first mentions of its cultus come from the year 1721. Painter Mikołaj Tereziński placed its short history under the original painting. Tereziński himself had gone blind and regained his sense of vision after praying to the Holy Mother. To express his gratitude he restored the Dubiecko image. Principal celebrations fall on the Feasts of the Sorrowful Mother (September 15) and the Immaculate Heart of the Virgin Mary (second Saturday after Corpus Christi).

Szczaworyż (Kielce Diocese), Our Lady of Szczaworyż. The picture is the altarpiece at St.Jacob's Church. Its cultus, which began in the 18th century, has continued until the present day. Principal celebration fall on the Feast of the Mother of the Church (second day of Pentecost).

Łódź, St. Adalbert's Church (Łódź Diocese), Madonna and Child. This late 17th century picture is the altarpiece at St. Adalbert's Church. Principal celebrations fall on the Feast of Our Lady of Consolation (Last Sunday in August).

Dobrzyków (Płock Diocese), Madonna and Child. This 17th century altarpiece at the Church of the Birthday of Our Lady is honoured by the faithful walking around it on their knees. Principal celebrations fall on the Birthday of Our Lady (September 8).

Kiszkowo (Gniezno Archdiocese), Madonna and Child . This 17th century painting is placed in St. John's Church. The first instance of cure was recorded in 1649. Principal celebrations fall on the Feast of Our Lady of Consolation (Last Sunday in August).

Lelów (Kielce Diocese), Madonna and Child also known as **Console of Lelów**. Placed in the Chapel of St. Martin's church, it is a copy of a greatly venerated painting burnt during World War II. Principal celebrations fall on the Feast of Our Lady of the Scapular (July 16).

Lgota Wielka (Częstochowa Diocese), Madonna and Child. It is the altarpiece at St. Clement's Church. First mentions of this widely venerated picture come from the 17th century. Principal celebrations fall on the Feast of Our Lady of the Rosary (October 7).

Płaza (Cracow Archdiocese), Our Lady of Consolation. This Baroque painting was described as miraculous in the 19th century records. Principal celebrations fall on the Feasts of Our Lady of the Angels (August 2) and Our Lady of Consolation (Sunday after August 28).

Łopacin (Płock Diocese), Our Lady of Łopacin. This altarpiece at the Church of the Birthday of Our Lady and St. Leonard is a copy of a 17th century image burnt in 1945. Principal celebrations fall on the Feast of the Birthday of Our Lady (September 8).

Błotnica (Sandomierz–Radom Diocese), Our Lady of Radom. The picture is the altarpiece at the Błotnica parish church. A local legend says that it was found by a ploughman from the nearby village of Ryki and offered to the church by the local landlord. Art critics ascribe this highly valuable late 14th century painting to the Italian School. It was most probably commissioned by the man whose likeness was painted in the lower left corner. The picture was strongly venerated already in the early 16th century. An inventory dated 1700 listed around 630 valuable votive offerings. Many people were miraculously cured at Błotnica, including the Bishop of Kiev, Józef Andrzej Załuski, the founder of the famous Załuski Library. Crowns were placed on the picture by Cardinal Karol Wojtyła soon before His elevation to the Holy See. Celebrations fall on the Feasts of The Mother of Church (2nd day of Pentecost), the Assumption (August 15) and the Birthday of Our Lady (September 8).

▶ **Binarowa (Tarnów Diocese), Madonna and Child**. A 17th century copy of the miraculous picture of Our Lady of the Sands from the Carmelite Church in Cracow. Some sources say that the picture was presented to the Binarowa Church by King John Casimir (1609—1672). Principal celebrations fall on the Feast of Our Lady, the Helper of the Faithful (May 24).

◀ **Staniątki (Cracow Archdiocese), The Sorrowful Mother (detail)**. The picture is placed at the Benedictine Convent Chapel. This oldest Polish Benedictine Convent is located on the outskirts of the Niepołomice Forest. The cultus of the Virgin Mary has been alive there for centuries. The original picture of the Holy Mother belonged to Abbess Wizenna. Among the famous people who prayed before it were Blessed Kinga, Blessed Salomea, Blessed Hedwig and Kings Ladislaus II Jagiełło (before the war against the Tutonic Knights), Boleslaus the Chaste, Sigismund the Old and John III Sobieski. The present 17th century picture is a copy of the painting of the Sorrowful Mother from the Franciscan Church in Cracow. The Virgin on the picture is pierced with seven swords. Four angels carrying the symbols of Christ's Passion are painted in the corners of this picture. It was crowned on September 21, 1924 by the Bishop of Cracow Adam Sapieha. Principal celebrations fall on the Feast of the Sorrowful Mother (August 15).

▶ **Gościeszyn (Gniezno Archdiocese), Our Lady of Gościeszyn**. The picture is the altarpiece at the Church of the Visitation. The Virgin and Child are presented on it in a mystical garden which is a rare way of depicting St. Mary in Polish art collections. This late 15th century Gothic work has some special features of the Netherlandish paintings. Some critics believe that it could have come from Dierick Bouts' workshop. Principal celebrations fall on the feasts of the Visitation (May 31) and the Birthday of Our Lady (September 8).

Ostrowąs (Włocławek Diocese), Our Lady of Ostrowąs. also known as **The Countess of Kujawy.** The picture is the altarpiece at the Church of the Birthday of Our Lady. A legend says that it was found in the early 17th century on a yew tree near an old, ruined wooden chapel. The news about the discovery quickly spread among the local people who began to gather before the Virgin's image which soon became known for its graces. The decision was then taken to move the picture to Brzeźno, 3 km away from Ostrowąs, and place it in a church which was just being built there. But, says an old story, the picture, gleaming with light, moved at night to the village of Plebanka from where, across a lake, it made its way to the same yew tree on which it had been found. The local people call the route covered by the picture "the Way of the Mother of God". This supernatural happening was interpreted as a manifestation of the Virgin's desire to have a church built near the yew tree. To comply with this wish, the local people heaped sand on the lake's bank forming a hill on which they raised a church in 1631. Principal celebrations fall on the Feast of the Birthday of Our Lady (September 8).

Tokarnia (Cracow Archdiocese), Madonna and Child also known as **Protector of Children**. This picture, which is the altarpiece at the wooden church of Our Lady of the Snows, comes from the late 17th century. It is particularly strongly venerated by mothers who use to bring their children to the Church to dedicate them to St. Mary. Prayers are said at Tokarnia on every first Sunday of each month for the killed, murdered, tortured and dead during Poland's millennial history. The shrine is also famous for annual Palm Sunday mystery plays during which the congregations carry several metre–high symbolic palms. Principal celebrations fall on the Feast of Our Lady of the Snows (August 5).

Licheń (Włocławek Diocese), Our Lady of Licheń also known as **The Sorrowful Queen of Poland**. The beginnings of the Cultus of St. Mary at Licheń date back to the mid–19th century. A roadside shrine brought from Częstochowa and placed in a nearby forest represented the Mother of God with a White Eagle emblem on her breasts.Her golden cloak was covered with symbols of Christ's Passion: the crown of thorns, whips, nails and spears. It was near that shrine that the Mother of God appeared to shepherd Mikołaj Sikatka in May 1850, and instructed him to encourage the people to improve and atone for their sins. She showed herself to him again on May 15 that year yet the people would not believe him. But two years later, when a dangerous cholera epidemic broke out at Licheń, a chapel was built in the place of the Virgin's appearance and a picture of Our Lady was placed there. Crowds of infected people gathered before it and many recovered, including some who were in critical condition. The epidemic died away. The Cultus of St. Mary flourished in Licheń afterwards. A procession carried the picture from the chapel to the parish church and in 1856 it was moved to a newly constructed church. Since 1949, the shrine has been taken care of by the Marist Friars. Our Lady of Licheń was crowned by Cardinal Stefan Wyszyński on August 15, 1967. He reminded on that occasion that he himself had been cured at Licheń from tuberculosis at the time he had still been an alumnus of the Włocławek Seminar. Celebrations fall on the Feast of the Assumption (August 15).

◄ **Stoczek Warmiński (Warmia Diocese), Our Lady of Stoczek** also known as **the Queen of Peace (detail)**. The picture is the altarpiece at the Church of the Visitation. At first the cultus focused on the statue of the Virgin Mary which was completely destroyed during the Reformation. The local church was also plundered then. After a new church was built, a picture of Our Lady of the Snows was placed there and the church was entrusted to the care of the Bernardine Monks. The sanctuary's recent history is connected with the Primate of the Millennium, Cardinal Stefan Wyszyński. After his imprisonment, Cardinal Wyszyński stayed at Stoczek Warmiński from October 12, 1953 to October 6, 1954. On December 8, 1953, he dedicated his life to the Virgin Mary. It was also at Stoczek that he first contemplated the idea of subjugating the Polish Nation to the Holy Mother in connection with the upcoming millennial anniversary of Poland's Baptism. On June 19, 1983, Pope John Paul II crowned the picture of the Queen of Peace during a ceremony at Częstochowa's Jasna Góra monastery. "By doing this, I want to thank the Mother of Peace for over three centuries of protection of the holy land of Warmia which, in spite of the twining roads of history, remained faithful to Christ and His Church". Principal celebrations fall on the Feasts of the Visitation (May 31), the Immaculate Conception (December 8), St. Ann (July 26), St. Francis (October 4) and St. Anthony (June 13).

▶ **Wieluń (Częstochowa Diocese), Madonna and Child**. The picture is placed at the Chapel of the Church of Corpus Christi. It was commissioned in 1640 from a Małopolska Painters' Guild by the Prior of the Augustian Monastery in Cracow, Father Stanislaw Starowski, which is evidenced by an inscription on the back of the picture. Covered by a silver robe, there is another inscription at the bottom of the picture which says: *Monstrate esse Matrem* (Show us that you are the Mother), and a kneeling figure of Father Starowski. The Confraternity of Our Lady of Consolation established at the Church in 1686 contributed to the development of Her cultus which was manifest in dedicating newly born babies to her motherly care. This custom has survived until the present day. On the Feast of Our Lady of Consolation ever year, the priest gives a special blessing to all children and the mothers entrust themselves to the Virgin's care.

Święta Lipka (Warmia Diocese), Our Lady of the Snows also known as **The Queen of Mazury**. The altarpiece at the Basilica of the Visitation of Our Lady to St. Elizabeth. The cultus of the Virgin Mary at Święta Lipka dates back to the 14th century when it was connected with a small figure placed on a lime tree, attracting numerous pilgrims. That figure disappeared at the time of the Reformation. The cultus was restored in the early 17th century, after the Jesuits arrived at Święta Lipka and brought with them the picture which at once became famous for miracles. It was painted by Flemish artist Bartholomew Pens and is a copy of the painting of Our Lady of the Snows from Santa Maria Maggiore Basilica in Rome. In the old times the people used to say: "What Częstochowa is for Poland and The Pointed Gate (*Ausros Vartai* or *Ostra Brama*) for Lithuania, Święta Lipka is for Warmia and Mazury. On August 11, 1968, the painting was crowned by Cardinal Stefan Wyszyński, the Primate of the Millennium. Principal celebrations at the Święta Lipka sanctuary fall on the Feasts of the Visitation (May 31), the Assumption (August 15) and the Birthday of Our Lady (September 8).

Miedzna (Siedlce Diocese), Our Lady of Miedzna. The picture is the altarpiece at the Church of the Annunciation. The origins of its cultus date back to 1724, the year when it was discovered beaming with unnatural light. The faithful experienced many miracles in its closeness. In 1730, following the painting's examination by an Ecclesiastical Commission, Bishop Rupniewski agreed to its being venerated in public. The church at Miedzna was burnt twice and only this picture survived each time, the fact which was interpreted as a confirmation of its miraculous powers. Water from a spring near the place where the picture was originally discovered is also said to have curative properties. Principal celebrations fall on the Feasts the Assumption (August 15), the Purification (February 2), the Annunciation (March 25), the Immaculate Conception (December 8) and Our Lady of the Scapular (July 16).

Wrocław Cathedral (Wrocław Archdiocese), Our Lady of Wrocław. The story of this picture is rather tangled. Some critics believe that is a work of known Italian painter Carlo Maratt (1625–1713) while some others consider it a copy of Giovanni Salvi's painting from the Uffizi in Florence. The picture was allegedly presented to King John III Sobieski (1629–1696) by Pope Innocent XI, the fact to which it owes the name of „Sobieski's Picture". But an inscription placed at its back is dated 1713 and bears the name of Aleksander Sobieski. To reconcile these versions the theory was formulated that the King had failed to collect the picture personally before his death and that it was eventually given to his son Aleksander by Pope Clement XI. In the mid–18th century the picture was placed at the parish church at Międzylesie, Lower Silesia, and in 1952 was brought to the Wrocław Cathedral of St. John the Baptist and placed in a side altar. Celebrations fall on the Feast of St. John the Baptist (June 24).

Piekary Śląskie (Katowice Diocese),

Our Lady of Piekary. The cultus of the Virgin Mary developed in Piekary already in the 15th century and the picture became famous throughout Silesia and Bohemia. After a plague broke out there in 1680, Emperor Leopold I asked the Bishop of Cracow to send the picture to Prague to deliver the city from annihilation. During the Swedish invasion, the Jesuits taking care of the sanctuary twice took the picture to Opole and eventually left it there. But it proved that its faithful copy also had miraculous powers and it is this copy which is now placed at the Church of St. Mary and St. Bartholomew in Piekary.

After 1890, the Way of the Cross imitating the original Calvary was built at Piekary attracting numerous pilgrimages. On August 15, 1925, the picture was crowned by Papal Nuncio Laurentio Lauri. In accordance with an old tradition, pilgrimages of men and youths from the Katowice Diocese arrive every last Saturday and Sunday of May at Piekary Śląskie which today is the most famous sanctuary in the whole of Upper Silesia. Before he was elected the Pope, Cardinal Karol Wojtyła had taken part in many such pilgrimages. In the Polish Liturgical Calendar, the Feast of Our Lady of Piekary falls on September 12.

Dobra (Tarnów Diocese), Madonna and Child. The beginnings of the cultus of the Virgin at Dobra, a village located in the beautiful landscape of Beskid Wyspowy Mts., date back to the 16th century. At that time, however, the cultus focused on a picture which was burnt when the local church went on fire. In 1692, Parish Priest Juraszewski ordered a new picture for the new church. This picture depicts Mary as she appeared to the Blessed Szymon Stock. It was commissioned by a man whose likeness is tucked in the lower right–hand corner of the picture. The cultus of the Madonna from Dobra has continued unimpaired since the end of the 17th century and has been propagated particularly strongly by the Confraternity of the Scapular. Principal celebrations fall on the Feast of Our Lady of the Scapular (July 16).

Jaśliska (Przemyśl Diocese), Our Lady of Jaśliska also known as **the Queen of Heaven and Earth**. This tempera picture painted on a 121 x 81 cm lime chalk-grounded panel is the altarpiece at the Church of St. Catherine. It is signed by Piotr Rafael Burnathowicz from Brzozów and dated 1634. But art critics, including Professor Juliusz Ros, tend to believe that it comes from the second half of the 16th century, which is confirmed by a mention of this picture in a 1602 inspection protocol. Most probably, Burnathowicz just restored the picture or repainted a part of it. According to Prof. Ros, the picture was initially of the rectangular shape and its upper part was rounded at a later date. Most probably the picture was brought to Jaśliska from Hungary by the Delipaczy family. The cultus of the Queen of Heaven and Earth has continued incessantly since the 17th century. Pilgrimages were undertaken to this shrine not only by Poles but also by Slovaks, Hungarians and Lemkas. Principal celebrations fall on the last Sunday of August, after the Feast of the Queen of the World (August 22).

127

Świdnica (Wrocław Archdiocese), Our Lady of Świdnica (detail). This 14th century panel painting is placed at St. Mary's Chapel at the Church of St. Stanislaus and St. Adalbert. The rays surrounding the Virgin's figure made the picture be sometimes called **Madonna in the Sun**. In 1459, it was placed in a chapel built at the cost of Świdnica butchers, the fact to which it owes the name of the Butchers' Chapel. During the 30 Years' War, the faithful took the picture away from the chapel and covered it with paint to protect it against desecration and destruction. Restored years later, it remains an object of veneration even though no special ceremonies take place at Świdnica on any of St.Mary's Feasts.

Ostrożany (Diocese in Drohiczyn), Madonna and Child. The picture is placed at the local Church of the Visitation of Our Lady to St. Elizabeth. According to a local legend, the Parish Church at Ostrożany is situated at the place where the Virgin Mary appeared to the local people among old lime trees. This miracle was confirmed by the impressions on the Virgin's feet on a stone which was next used as the base of the altar at the Church. The picture itself most probably comes from the early 16th century. It was generally venerated at that time. In 1661 the Confraternity of the Rosary was founded at Ostrożany. The painting was crowned by Cardinal Józef Glemp on July 5, 1987. Principal celebrations fall on the Feast of the Birthday of Our Lady (September 8).

Ostrowo (Gniezno Archdiocese), Our Lady of the Scapular. This late 15th century painting on an oak panel is generally ascribed to the Dutch school. The extraordinary background and the transparent muslin veil, which covers the Child and which is so delicate that it is hardly visible, deserve special attention. Intense cultus of St. Mary, which began in the 18th century, declined at the time of Poland's partitioning and today it is local in character. Principal celebrations fall on the Feast of Our Lady of the Scapular (July 16).

Limanowa (Tarnów Diocese), Our Lady of Limanowa. This 14th century Gothic Pieta, placed at the Church of the Sorrowful Mother, is a work of an ananonymous folk sculptor. It was probably brought to Poland from Hungary or Slovakia. At first it was venerated at a roadside chapel at the village of Mordarka, from where it was moved to Limanowa in 1774. Its centuries' long cultus flourished particularly strongly during World Wars I and II. The local people believe that the Sorrowful Mother several times

saved the church and the whole town from destruction. The figure was crowned on September 11, 1966, the year marking Poland's millennium, by the Cracow Metropolitan Bishop, Karol Wojtyła. The crowns were stolen in 1981 and during his pilgrimage to Poland in 1983, Pope John Paul II crowned the Limanowa Pieta again. Three–day celebrations are held at the shrine in connection with the Feast of the Sorrowful Mother (September 15).

▶ Pieta (detail)

◀ **Powsin (Warsaw Archdiocese), Our Lady of Powsin** also known as **The Longing Mary**. This mid–17th century picture is the altarpiece at St. Elizabeth's Church. A post–visitation protocol dated 1675 refers to it as a miraculous image and mentions many votive offerings placed at its side. Its cultus has survived until the present day although it now is of a local character. Principal celebrations fall on the Feast of the Assumption (August 15).

▶ **Popowice (Częstochowa Diocese), Our Lady of Charity.** The picture is placed in the central altar of the Church of All Saints. It is ascribed to the 17th century Italian School. What is interesting in this picture is the fact that although the child on St. Mary's knees is still just a little baby, the Virgin is shedding tears of blood as if anticipating her son's crucifixion. Principal celebrations fall on the feast of the Sorrowful Mother (September 15).

◀ **Myślenice (Cracow Archdiocese), Madonna and Child** also known as **Our Lady of Myślenice (detail)**. The picture is placed at the chapel of the Church of the Birthday of Our Lady. This magnificent image from the late 16th century belonged to Pope Sixtus V who presented it on his death bed in 1590 to his sister. In turn, she gave it to the Cracow Castellan, Prince Jerzy Zbarski, who brought it to Poland in 1596. When a plague broke out in Cracow thirty years later, the people used to carry out all their belongings to the streets and burn them. The same became of Prince Zbarski's possessions. The picture was saved by Marcin Grabysza, the Prince's clerk from Myślenice. In 1692 he brought the painting to his hometown. Four years later, traces of tears were detected on its surface and many people, including Grabysza himself, were cured before it. The cultus of Our Lady of Myślenice has flourished ever since. In August 1969 the picture was crowned by the then Metropolitan Bishop of Cracow, Cardinal Karol Wojtyła. Celebrations fall on the Feast of the Birthday of Our Lady (September 8).

Narew (Diocese in Drohiczyn), Our Lady of the Scapular (detail). Little is known about the history of this 17th century altarpiece from the Church of St. Stanislaus. But its cultus had to be intense, which is illustrated by numerous votive offerings placed on the painting. Principal celebrations fall on the Feast of Our Lady of the Scapular (Sunday after July 16).

▶ **Gietrzwałd (Warmia Diocese), Our Lady of Warmia (detail)**. The first mention of this early 16th century image comes from the year 1505. It is a copy of Our Lady of Częstochowa. The Gietrzwałd sanctuary owes its fame to miraculous appearances of the Holy Mother between June 27 and September 16, 1877. She first showed herself to a 13 years old girl, Justyna Szafrańska, among the branches of a maple tree near the local parish church. The girl, who was just preparing herself for the First Holy Communion, experienced the same miracle several times afterwards and sometime later the Holy Mother appeared to her friend, 12 years old Barbara Samułowska. On September 10, 1967, the image was crowned by Cardinal Stefan Wyszyński, and ten years later, on the 100th anniversary of the appearances, a Congress devoted to St. Mary was held at Gietrzwałd. Principal celebrations fall on the Feasts of the Visitation (September 8), the Assumption (August 15), the Birthday of Our Lady (September 8) and the Immaculate Conception (December 8).

Kalisz – Niedźwiady (Włocławek Diocese), Our Lady of Perpetual Help. In the late 19th century the picture was brought from Rome to the Barefoot Carmelite Nuns' Convent in Lvov, where it was generally venerated by the faithful. When they were leaving Lvov after the war, the nuns took the picture with them as the most priceless treasure and placed in the central altar of their Convent Chapel in Kalisz—Niedźwiady. Principal celebrations fall on the Feast of Our Lady of Perpetual Help (June 27).

Pasierbiec (Tarnow Diocese). Our Lady of Consolation. This anonymous 19th century picture of Our Lady of Consolation bears traces of the local folklore. One interesting iconographic motif is the presentation of the Virgin against the image of God. Principal celebrations fall on the first Saturday after the Feast o St. Augustine (August 28).

▶ **Włościejewki (Poznań Diocese), Madonna and Child (detail).** A tempera panel paining from the early 16th century portraying the Virgin as an apocalyptic figure wrapped in the sun and adored by angels. An interesting legend is connected with the construction of the late Gothic church at Włościejewki. Passed from generation to generation, it says that the Virgin Mary showed herself to workers building the church and left the impression of her feet on a stone. The stone was placed in the Church's wall. Pilgrims arriving at this shrine kiss this impression with great devotion. Principal celebrations fall on the Feast of Our Lady of the Scapular (July 16).

ECO DORMIO SED COR MEVN VIGILLAT

Wyszyna (Włocławek Diocese), Our Lady Adoring the Infant Jesus also known as **Our Lady of Wyszyna**. The picture is the altarpiece at the Church of the Birthday of Our Lady. According to a local legend, the veneration of this picture began with the following event. One day, Father Feliks Rydzyński from the Order of the Reformati was anointing a dying man from Koło. He told him to repeat: *Monstra Te esse Matrem* (Show me that you are the Mother). When the friar left the sick man alone for a while, a painting, which was hanging on the wall, suddenly moved into the dying man's hands. This event was considered to have been a sign of God and the Holy Mother and the picture was moved to the Church at Wyszyna where it soon became famous for miracles. Numerous pilgrimages were arriving at Wyszyna and the graces attributed to the Virgin were described in a special book. Principal celebrations fall on the Feasts of Our Lady of the Scapular (Sunday after July16) and the Birthday of Our Lady (September 8).

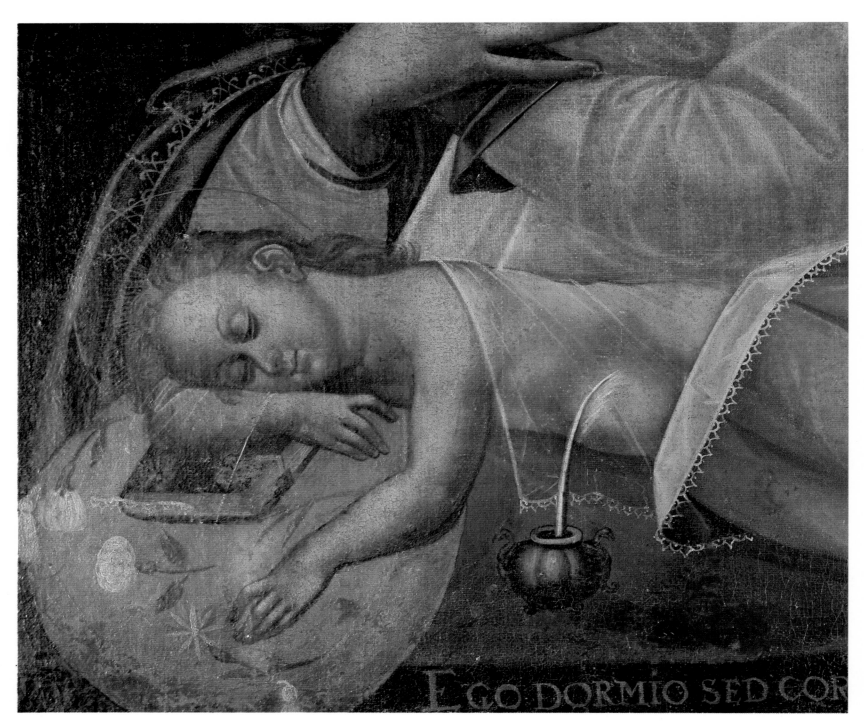

Our Lady of Wyszyna (detail)

▶ Our Lady of Wyszyna (detail)

Warsaw (Warsaw Archdiocese), Our Lady of Berdyczów. also known as **Kresowa Hetmanka.** The picture, placed in a side chapel of the Church of Victorious Mother of God, is a faithful copy of the picture of Our Lady of Berdyczów venerated for centuries in the whole of the Ukraine, Volhynia and Podolia. Her cultus could be compared to those of the Jasna Góra or the Pointed Gate (*Ausros Vartai* or *Ostra Brama*) Madonnas. The copy found in Warsaw is said to have once belonged to a famous Carmelite, Father Marek, the central figure of Juliusz Slowacki's drama *Ksiądz Marek*. It was also the altarpiece in the field altar of the Bar Confederates (1768–1772). Principal Celebrations fall on the Feast of the Assumption (August 15).

Żuromin (Płock Diocese), Our Lady of Żuromin. The picture is the altarpiece at St.Anthony's Church. It depicts a scene from the life of St.Anthony who is handed the Child by Holy Mother. It is traditionally believed that the picture was brought to Żuromin by an unknown soldier in the early 18th century. At first, it was placed in the house of a pious peasant by the name of Bloch, and it was there that the first supernatural events were recorded. For instance, in 1708, the picture started gleaming with unnatural light and drops of some unknown liquid appeared on its surface. The painting was moved to the Church where the cultus of the Virgin Mary developed on a broad scale. Precious Baroque votive offerings, the oldest of which date back to 1731, have been preserved at the Church. Principal celebrations fall on the Feast of the Birthday of Our Lady (September 8).

Wieliczka (Cracow Archdiocese), Our Lady of Grace.
This is a rare example of a picture painted directly on stone. It comes from the second half of the 17th century. A legend says that the Wieliczka miners commissioned the picture and placed in the local salt mine's shaft of St. Elizabeth. But since the air was very humid there and the picture was exposed to destructive influence of salt, the miners presented it to the Order of the Reformati. Celebrations fall on the Feast of Our Lady of the Angels (August 2).

Dębe (Włocławek Diocese), Madonna and Child. A late 15th century altarpiece at the Church of the Annunciation. Its cultus developed quickly. Votive offerings from the early 17th century have been preserved at the Church. The Bishop of Gniezno, Gabriel Podolski, issued a decree in 1771, in which he confirmed the painting's miraculous powers. Today the cultus is of local character. Principal celebrations fall on the Feast of the Annunciation (March 25) and Pentecost.

▶ **Warsaw, Jesuit Church (Warsaw Archdiocese), Our Lady of Grace, the Patron of Warsaw**. This 17th century painting by an unknown artist from the Venetian School is a copy of the famous Our Lady of Grace from Faenza. It was brought to Warsaw from Rome in 1651 by Papal Nuncio Giovanni de Torres as a sign of Pope Inocent X's blessing for King John Casimir (1609–1672). It was at first placed at the Piarist Church and in 1834 was moved to the Jesuit Church. During the great plague which broke out in Warsaw in 1664, processions were carrying the painting around the city. Since the plague ended quickly it was generally believed that a miracle had happened and to commemorate it similar processions were organised on every second Sunday in May until the time of Poland's partitioning by foreign powers. Cardinal Stefan Wyszyński decorated the picture with Papal crowns on October 7, 1973. Principal celebrations fall on the Feast of Our Lady of Grace (May 9).

◀ **Gostyń (Poznań Archdiocese), Our Lady of Gostyń** also known as **the Rose of Święta Góra**. It is the altarpiece at the Plilippian Friars Church located outside the town on a hill known as Święta Góra. The church itself was built to resemble the famous Venetian Santa Maria della Salute. At first, a Gothic polychromed Pieta, now placed in a side altar, was venerated at Gostyń. But around the 17th century the cultus focused on the Virgin's picture. The Pieta was crowned by Cardinal August Hlond on June 24, 1928. Święta Góra is at present one of the main religious centres of struggle against alcoholism. According to the Polish liturgical calendar, the Feast of Our Lady of Gostyń falls on June 25. Other principal celebrations are held on the Feasts of the Assumption (August 15), the Birthday of Our Lady (8 September) and the Immaculate Conception (December 8).

Sobótka (Sandomierz–Radom Diocese), Madonna and Child. The picture, which is the altarpiece at St. Margaret's Church, is a copy of the famous *La Madonna miraculosa di San Marco* from St. Mark's Basilica in Venice. It was brought to Sobótka in the 1870s. An inscription on this 98 cm x 72 cm oil painting on a double canvas tells that the original, which is said to have contributed to the victories of its owners Emperors Justinian I and Alexander I, was painted by St. Luke. Its copy in Sobótka has been venerated for over a hundred years now, which is evidenced by a big number of votive offerings and entries in the Book of Graces. Principal celebrations fall on the Feasts of the Victorious Madonna (October 7).

Kalisz (Włocławek Diocese), The Holy Family. The picture is placed at the chapel of the Collegiate Church of the Assumption and St. Joseph. TheCollegiate Church in Kalisz, Poland's oldest town, is probably the only place throughout the world where the cultus of the Holy Mother develops together with that of her betrothed St. Joseph. This cultus has developed incessantly since the mid–18th century. At a ceremony held on May 15, 1796, Papal Crowns were placed with Pope Pius VI's permission not onlyon the heads of Mary and Jesus but also on the head of Joseph, who one hundred years later was proclaimed the Patron of the Kujawy–Kalisz Diocese. Since the end of WorldWar II, the clergymen, who had been inmates of the Dachau Nazi concentration camp, have made traditional pilgrimages to the Kalisz Church. In April 1945, the Nazis decided to liquidate the camp and the inmates, many of whom were priests from Poland, faced death. One of them encouraged the other prisoners to pray to Our Lady and St. Joseph of Kalisz. The camp was eventually liberated just several hours before the expected execution. Ever since, the priests from Dachau have made annual thanksgiving pilgrimages to the Kalisz sanctuary. Principal celebrations fall on the Feasts of St. Joseph (March 19) and the Assumption (August 15).

Wojkowice (Częstochowa Diocese), Our Lady of the Good Way. Art critics believe that this beautiful picture was painted in Małopolska between 1460 and 1470. It is placed at the Church of St. Bartholomew situated along the Warsaw–Katowice highway. It was probably for this reason that the Bishop of Częstochowa, Stanisław Nowak, wrote the following entry in the Wojkowice parish records: „On the Feast of the Immaculate Heart of Our Lady, I blessed the restored painting and proclaimed Wojkowice the Sanctuary of Our Lady of the Good Way. May She protect this Parish as well as all the people travelling along local roads and highways". The title of Our Lady of the Good Way is the only such title in the sanctuaries of St. Mary in Poland.

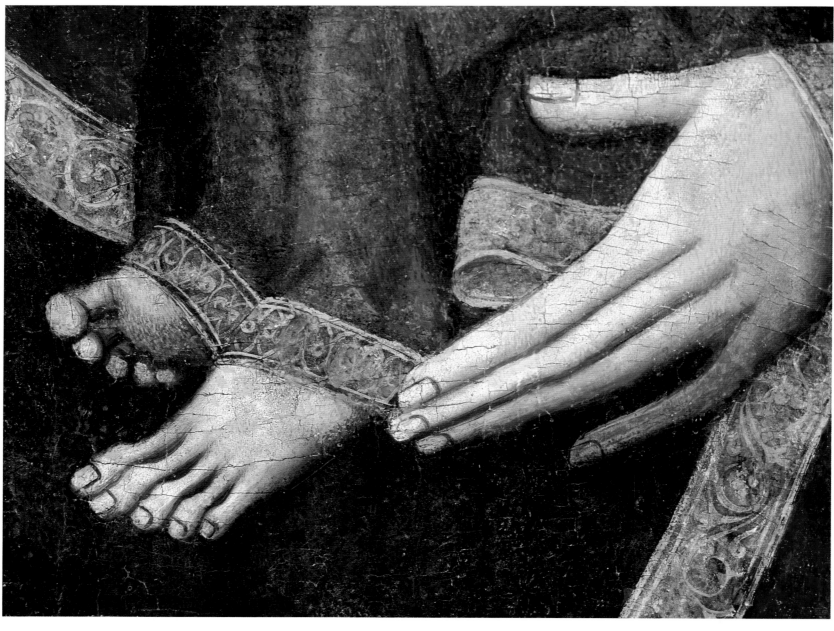

Copies of the Miraculous Image of Our Lady of Częstochowa.

The eminent role played by Our Lady of Jasna Góra and Her cultus is evidenced by big numbers of widely distributed copies of the original painting. In 1981 and 1982 all-Polish plein air art exhibitions were organised, featuring over 260 works illustrating new trends in sacral art. During the past six centuries, the cultus of the Black Madonna Icon was manifest in the arts and in folklore, in symbolic iconography, legends, songs and customs. The copies of the image of Our Lady of Częstochowa are an extension of this cultus. First such copies were painted in the 15th century. With the passage of time, and especially in the 19th century, their number kept growing quickly. There are two kinds. of Black Madonna's presentation. The first consists in copying faithfully the original, while the second belongs to the iconographic category of St. Mary, the Queen of Poland. The 1621 Cracow Synod instructed Polish painters to keep close to the Jasna Góra model to preserve the canon of St. Mary's presentation. Since 1957, one and the same copy of Our Lady of Jasna Góra has been travelling throughout Poland, visiting homes in even the most distant parishes.

▶ **Bochnia (Tarnów Diocese).** This picture, dating back to the late 15th or early 16th century, was probably painted by the same artists who restored the image from Jasna Góra. Tears of blood and traces of sweat were found on the surface of the Bochnia painting between the years 1632 and 1638. This fact gave rise to the picture's great cultus. The crowning ceremony took place in October 1934. Principal celebrations fall on the Feast of Our Lady of the Rosary (first Sunday in October).

Index

▶ **Przemyśl–Prałkowce (Przemyśl Diocese),** This 16th century painting was brought to the Church of Our Lady, the Queen of Poland after World War II from Zbaraż, Volhynia where it had been greatly venerated at the Bernardine Monks' Monastery. Among the famous people who said prayers before it were Prince Jeremia Wiśniowiecki (1612—1651) and Kings John Casimir (1609—1672) and Michał Korybut (1640—1673). Principal celebrations fall on the Feast of the Assumption (August 15).

▶▶ **Cracow, St. Mary's Church (Cracow Archdiocese).** This copy of Our Lady of Częstochowa comes from the first half of the 17th century, i.e., from the time when the Cracow Synod (1621) issued the instruction that the images of the Virgins hould follow the Częstochowa model. The picture is placed in the retable of the Solomons' Chapel located beneath the Church's lower tower. The picture was crowned by Cardinal Stefan Wyszyński on December 15, 1968. Principal celebrations fall on the Feast of the Assumption (August 15).

▶ **Zgłowiączki (Włocławek Diocese), Madonna and Child.** It is the altarpiece at the Church of the Birthday of Our Lady. The picture was most strongly venerated in the 19th century, the time when numerous pilgrimages were arriving at the Zgłowiączki sanctuary. Celebrations fall on the Feast of the Visitation (May 31).

Koziebrody (Płock Diocese). This copy of Our Lady of Częstochowa comes from the 17th century. Its cultus was confirmed during a canonical visitation in 1785. Around a hundred 18th century votive plaques have been preserved around the image until the present day. Principal celebrations fall on the Feast of the Birthday of Our Lady (September 8).

◀◀**Topczewo (Diocese in Drohiczyn).**
This image of Madonna and Child is placed at the Church of St. Stanislaus. Painted in the 17th century, it was damaged during the Swedish invasion (cut into 76 pieces). It was restored some time later but the cuts are well visible on the canvas. Many miracles were attributed to this image and their fame even reached Jasna Góra where they are described in the Monastery's archive records. Principal celebrations fall on the Feast of Our Lady of Częstochowa (August 26).

◀**Wierzchlas (Częstochowa Diocese).**
A 1668 post–visitation protocol says that the local church contains a painting of Our Lady of Częstochowa decorated with two sliver gold–plated crowns and 19 votive offerings. Many cures and miracles were recorded at Wierzchlas. Principal celebrations fall on the Feast of the Assumption (August 15).

◀**Chyliczki (Warsaw Archdiocese).** The painting is placed in the chapel of a former school for girls in St. Ann's Parish at Piaseczno near Warsaw. It was gifted to the school by Father Reyman, the Prior of the Pauline Monastery.

Sandomierz, Church of the Holy Spirit (Sandomierz–Radom Diocese). The people of Sandomierz commissioned this image after World War II to thank Our Lady for the town's miraculous deliverance. From the beginning it has been an object of intense veneration.

▶ **Giebułtów (Cracow Archdiocese), Madonna and Child**. The picture is the altarpiece at the Church of St. Giles. It is a feretory painting and every year a procession is held during which it is carried out of the Church. Field masses held on these occasions attract thousands of people.

▶ **Ogrodzieniec (Kielce Diocese), Our Lady of the Rock**. Its name comes from this sanctuary's unusual location on a lime rock several metres above a small field chapel at which Holy Masses are said every Sunday. The image was placed so high because water from a spring below was believed to have miraculous curative properties. Principal celebrations fall on Pentecost.